GIFTED & TALENTED®

To develop your child's gifts and talents

MATH

Written by Tracy Masonis
Larry Martinek, Math Consultant

McGraw Hill Children's Publishing

Columbus, Ohio

Dear Parents,

Gifted & Talented Math has been designed specifically to promote the development of critical and creative thinking skills. The activities in this book include visual puzzles, logic problems, riddles, and more. All of the activities will spark your child's imagination, sharpen thinking skills, and foster a love of learning.

The activities in this book have been organized according to topics and skills outlined in current math standards. They are intended to reinforce and extend the math concepts your child has already been introduced to at school or at home. For example, in the section on operations and computation, your child will need to apply the concepts of addition and subtraction to solve a variety of challenging problems.

Some of the activities have been grouped so that they give your child practice using a certain type of thinking strategy. For example, two logic problems may be placed side by side so that when your child figures out how to solve the first one, he or she may apply those skills to solve the second one. Each problem, however, can stand alone and does not have to be done in any particular order.

Most of the problems can be completed directly on the workbook pages. In some instances, though, your child might prefer to use a separate sheet of paper to figure out the answers. For certain pages, suggestions are given for using coins and other manipulatives to help your child solve the problems.

While working in this book, your child may be inspired by the activities to create his or her own problems. If so, have your child present the problems to you and explain the answers. Praise your child's efforts and encourage him or her to continue making more problems and puzzles. This type of activity not only stimulates creativity, but it also deepens your child's understanding of mathematical concepts and increases the ability to reason mathematically.

 Children's Publishing

Send all inquiries to:
McGraw-Hill Children's Publishing
8787 Orion Place
Columbus, OH 43240-4027

ISBN 1-57768-944-5

1 2 3 4 5 6 7 8 9 10 VHG 08 07 06 05 04 03

The **McGraw-Hill** Companies

Table of Contents

Number Sense

Operations and Computation

Number Patterns

Fractions

Logical Thinking

Survey Says!

Pick at least 10 people (family or friends) for a survey.

Find out how many people:

_____ watch no TV

_____ watch 1–2 hours per day

_____ watch 3–4 hours per day

_____ watch more than 4 hours per day

Record the ages of the people in each group above.

_____ under 10 years old

_____ 10–15 years old

_____ 16–20 years old

_____ over 20 years old

Record the information in the chart below.

	0 hours	1–2 hours	3–4 hours	over 4 hours
under 10 years old				
10–15				
16–20				
over 20				

Take a good look at your chart. Can you draw any conclusions about which age group is most likely to watch 2 to 3 hours of TV per day? Explain your answer.

_____

_____

Survey Says It Again!

Pick at least 10 people
(family or friends) for a survey.

Find out how many people:

_____ do not use the Internet

_____ use the Internet 1–2 hours per day

_____ use the Internet 3–4 hours per day

_____ use the Internet more than 4 hours per day

Record the sex of the people in each group above.

_____ males _____ females

Record the information in the chart b.elow.

	0 hours	1-2 hours	3-4 hours	over 4 hours
male				
female				

Take a good look at your table. What conclusions can you draw about Internet use?

Explain your answer. _____

_____

_____

Miles and Miles of Miles and Miles!

The Earth is about 93,000,000 miles from the Sun.

Pluto is about 3,700,000,000 miles from the Sun.

Jupiter is about 483,000,000 miles from the Sun.

The moon is about 240,000 miles from the Earth.

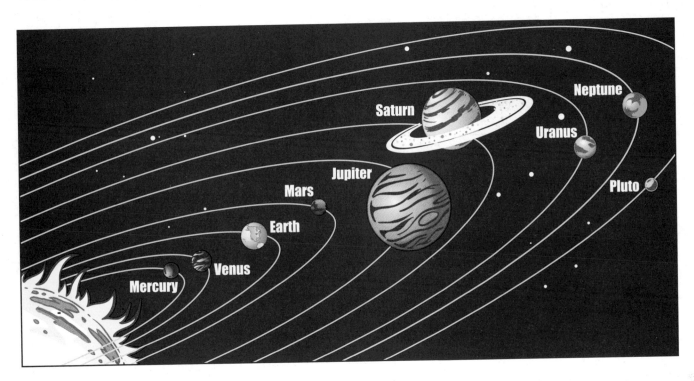

Which planet is closest to the Sun? _____

Which planet is farthest from the Sun? _____

Arrange the four numbers above in order from smallest to largest.

_____   _____

_____   _____

Name _____

A year is 365 days long. A week is 7 days. Months can have 28, 29, 30, or 31 days. A fortnight is 14 days. A decade is either 3,652 or 3,653 days.

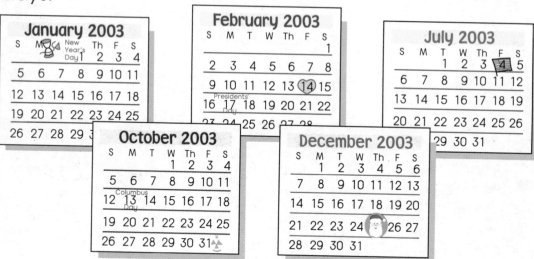

Arrange the numbers above in order from smallest to largest.

_____

_____

_____

_____

_____

_____

_____

Round Up (and Down)!

A rancher has 73 cows. Would it be more accurate to say he has "about 70 cows" or that he has "about 80 cows"?

Circle your answer: about 70   about 80

Another rancher has 278 sheep. Would it be more accurate to say he has "about 200 sheep" or that he has "about 300 sheep"? Round to the nearest hundred.

Circle your answer: about 200   about 300

Round and Round!

A mile is 5,280 feet. Round to the nearest thousand.

Circle your answer: 4,000   5,000   6,000

A dancer spins around twice. Each spin is 360 degrees. To the nearest hundred, how many degrees did the dancer spin?

Circle your answer:

600   700   800

Mental Math!

Add the following numbers in your head:

199 + 36 = _____

200 + 147 = _____

250 + 75 = _____

375 + 126 = _____

Subtract the following numbers in your head:

200 – 10 = _____

300 – 23 = _____

400 – 101 = _____

250 – 151 = _____

Compute:

1 + 2 + 3 + 4 + 5 + 6 + 7 + 8 + 9 + 10 = _____

10 + 20 + 30 + 40 + 50 + 60 + 70 + 80 + 90 + 100 = _____

10 – 9 + 8 – 7 + 6 – 5 + 4 – 3 + 2 – 1 = _____

100 – 90 + 80 – 70 + 60 – 50 + 40 – 30 + 20 – 10 = _____

Sums and Differences

Compute. Show your work.

$1 + 23 + 456 + 7,890 = $ _____

$2,000 - 456 = $ _____

$1 + 100 + 10 + 1,000 + 10,000 = $ _____

$3,000,000 - 234,567 = $ _____

$2,345 - 400 + 399 = $ _____

$369 + 725 - 368 = $ _____

Close Enough Is Good Enough!

An estimate is an answer that is close to the exact answer. It is a "rough calculation" when the exact answer is not needed.

For example, Billy saved $12 the first week, $19 the next week, and $ 25 this week. Does he have enough money to buy a skateboard that costs $100? Don't calculate—**estimate**.

Circle your answer:

    Yes, he has enough.

    No, he does not have enough.

Explain your answer:

_____

Joan has $ 303. She buys a coat that costs $106. About how much money does she have left?

_____

Close Enough Is Still Good Enough!

Estimate the answers below to the nearest ten. Do **not** work out the exact answer.

341 + 52 = _____

341 − 52 = _____

667 + 125 = _____

667 − 125 = _____

511 + 495 = _____

511 − 495 = _____

407 + 291 = _____

407 − 291 = _____

234 + 379 + 99 + 305 = _____

2,989 + 34 + 5,102 + 899 = _____

10,000 − 2,001 − 4,981 − 999 − 1,005 = _____

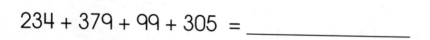

Mental Math!

Multiply the following numbers in your head:

4 x 125 = _____

5 x 64 = _____

10 x 37 = _____

100 x 432 = _____

Divide the following numbers in your head:

200 ÷ 50 = _____   300 ÷ 2 = _____

400 ÷ 4 = _____   150 ÷ 25 = _____

Compute. Show your work.

12,345,679 x 8 = _____

6,420,864 ÷ 2 = _____

More Mental Math!

Multiply the following numbers in your head:

8 x 225 = _____

10 x 420 = _____

50 x 60 = _____

100 x 360 = _____

Divide the following numbers in your head:

1,000 ÷ 50 = _____   300 ÷ 20 = _____

4,000 ÷ 40 = _____   2,500 ÷ 250 = _____

Compute. Show your work.

12,345,679 x 27 = _____

18,200 ÷ 14 = _____

Calculate This!

Name _____

A **light year** is how far a beam of light travels in one year. Light travels about 186,000 miles per second. To calculate how many miles are in a light year, you have to multiply the number of seconds in a year by 186,000.

The problem is that most calculators hold only 8 digits, and the answer has 13 digits!

Your mission: Figure out how to multiply 60 x 60 x 24 x 365 x 186,000 on a calculator and get the **exact answer**!

What is the answer? _____

How did you figure it out?

_____

_____

Give Them an Inch

Name _____

There are 12 inches in a foot and 5,280 feet in a mile. Use a calculator to figure out how many half-inches there are in a mile.

1 mile
5,280 feet
? inches

Use your calculator to do the following problems:

12,345,679 x 9 = _____

12,345,679 x 18 = _____

12,345,679 x 27 = _____

12,345,679 x 36 = _____

Do you see the pattern? Without using your calculator, what is:

12,345,679 x 72 = _____

12,345,679 x ____ = 555,555,555

Darling Decimals!

Oh, those darling decimals! They can be tricky! When working with decimals, it often is helpful to think what we know about money.

For example, 7 + 1.25 can be thought of as $7.00 + $1.25, and 6.7 - 2.65 can be thought of as $6.70 - $2.65.

Calculate. Show your work.

3 + 4.56 = _____   5.67 + 3.9 = _____

12.3 + 3.12 = _____   15.67 + 123 = _____

8 – 2.25 = _____   12.75 – 3.2 = _____

7 – 4.56 = _____   12.3 – 4 = _____

Add and Subtract Those Decimals!

Calculate. Show your work.

12 + 4.96 + 23.9 + 7 = _____

23 − 4.96 − 2.1 − 5 = _____

4.1 + 2.48 − 2 − 1.3 = _____

99 − 5.2 + 7.41 − 12 = _____

The Next Number, Please!

Write the next three numbers in each of the following number patterns:

1, 2, 4, 7, 11, _____, _____, _____

1, 11, 10, 20, 19, _____, _____, _____

1, 2, 4, 8, 16, _____, _____, _____

1, 4, 9, 16, 25, _____, _____, _____

0, 1, 1, 2, 3, 5, 8, 13, _____, _____, _____

32, 16, 8, 4, 2, _____, _____, _____

Next. . .!

Write the next three numbers in each of the following number patterns:

0, $1\frac{1}{2}$, 3, $4\frac{1}{2}$, 6, _____, _____, _____

1, 3, 7, 15, 31, _____, _____, _____

1, 11, 10, 20, 19, _____, _____, _____

5, 10, 20, 40, 80, _____, _____, _____

25, 20, 15, 10, _____, _____, _____

0, 5, 15, 35, 75, 155, _____, _____, _____

Picture This!

Answer each question. Then draw a figure that completes each group.

What is the same about each figure? _____

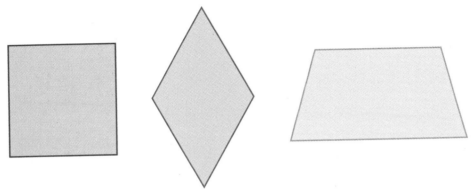

What is the same about each figure? _____

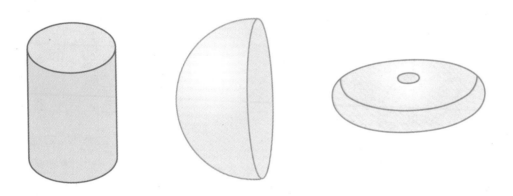

What is the same about each figure? _____

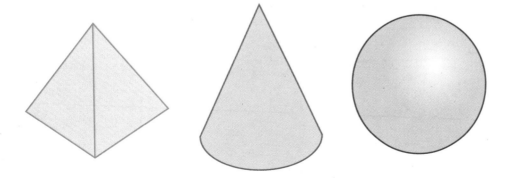

You Belong to Me!

Name _____

Cross out the figure that **does not** belong with the others.

What is the same about each figure? _____

   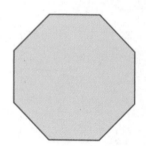

Cross out the figure that **does not** belong with the others.

What is the same about each figure? _____

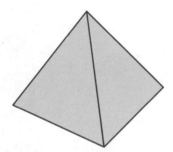  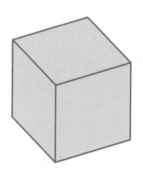 

Cross out the figure that **does not** belong with the others.

What is the same about each figure? _____

   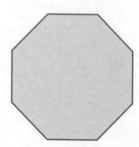

Help Harpo, Henrietta, and Hank!

Help Harpo figure out the total value of the coins in his piggy bank.

Find the total value of the coins in the picture.

Total = $ _____ . _____

Help Henrietta figure out the total value of the coins in her piggy bank.

Find the total value of the coins in the picture.

Total = $ _____ . _____

Help Hank figure out the total value of the coins and bills in his shoe box.

Find the total value of the bills and coins in the picture.

Total = $ _____ . _____

Missing Money!

Name _____

Harpo's sister, Hanna, decided to count the money in her change purse and her piggy bank.

Find the total value of the bills and coins shown in the picture.

Total = $ _____._____

Hanna has a problem. The last time she counted the money from her piggy bank, she put a note on it saying, "This bank contains only dimes and quarters. It contains a total of $4.50. There are 10 quarters and _____ dimes."

The problem is that the number of dimes got smudged out. Without actually counting the coins, how can Hanna figure out how many dimes are in the bank?

This bank contains only dimes and quarters. It contains a total of $4.50. There are 10 quarters and 🐭 dimes.

Number of dimes = _____

Explain how you found your answer.

_____

_____

_____

One for the Money!

After every five tickets are sold, the ticket seller at the carnival records the amount of money he has taken in so far. Look at his chart below:

Tickets	5	10	15	20	25	30	35	40	45	50
Total	$12.50	$25.00	$37.50							

After 25 tickets are sold, how much money will be recorded in the chart?

Total = $ _____ . _____

After 40 tickets are sold, how much money will be recorded in the chart?

Total = $ _____ . _____

After 50 tickets are sold, how much money will be recorded in the chart?

Total = $ _____ . _____

More for the Money!

After every five tickets are sold, the ticket seller at the carnival records the amount of money he has taken in so far. Look at his chart below:

Tickets	5	10	15	20	25	30	35	40	45	50
Total	$12.50	$25.00	$37.50							

Fill in the chart.

How much does one ticket cost?

one ticket = $ _____ . _____

After 32 tickets are sold, how much money will have been taken in?

Total = $ _____ . _____

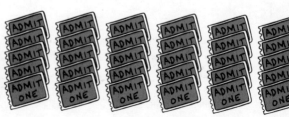

Name _____

Red, White, and Blue!

Half of the marbles in a bag are red.
A quarter of the marbles are white.
The rest are blue.

What fractional part of the marbles
is blue? _____

If six of the marbles are blue, how many are white? _____

How many total marbles are there in the bag? _____

Twelve blue marbles are
added to the bag. What
fractional part of the
marbles is now blue?

_____

What fractional part of
the marbles is now white?

_____

Straight From the Horse's Mouth!

A furlong is a unit of measure used mostly in horse racing. A furlong is one-eighth ($\frac{1}{8}$) of a mile.

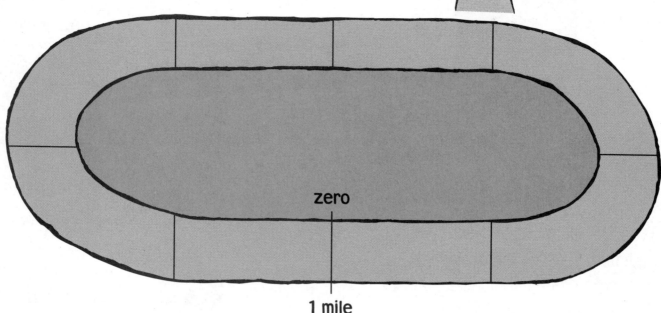

zero

1 mile

What fractional part of a mile is 4 furlongs? _____

What fractional part of a mile is 6 furlongs? _____

What fractional part of a mile is $7\frac{1}{2}$ furlongs? _____

How many furlongs are in $\frac{1}{4}$ of a mile? _____

How many furlongs are in $1\frac{3}{16}$ of a mile? _____

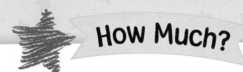

How Much?

Half-of-a-quarter of a piece of cheese weighs 6 ounces. How much does the whole piece weigh?

Total weight = _____ ounces = _____ pounds

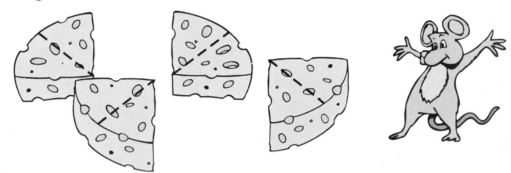

A sandbox is half full. When 200 pounds of sand are added, the box contains 750 pounds of sand. How much sand will the sandbox hold?

The sandbox will hold _____ pounds of sand.

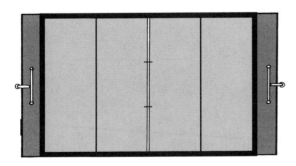

How much of the football game is left half way through the second quarter? _____

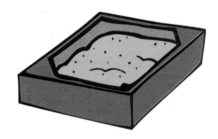

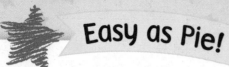
Papa bear ate a quarter of the whole pie. Mama bear ate one-third of the remaining pie. Baby bear ate half of what was left.

How much of the pie did Papa bear eat? _____

How much of the pie did Mama bear eat? _____

How much of the pie did Baby bear eat? _____

How much of the pie was left for Goldilocks? _____

Logic It Out!

Three times a certain number, minus 1, equals 32. Find the number.

$$3 \times \underline{\qquad} - 1 = 32$$

The number of bacteria in a jar doubles every day. After 20 days, the jar is full. When was the jar half full?

The jar was half full on the _____ day.

Who is the better free-throw shooter, Freddie or Jamie?

Freddie made 17 out of 24 free throws.

Jamie made 8 out of 12 free throws.

_____ is the better shooter.

Explain your answer.

_____

_____

_____

The distance from City 1 to City 2 is 100 miles. The distance from City 2 to City 3 is 25 miles.

City 1

City 2

What is the **maximum** distance possible between City 1 and City 3?

Maximum distance = _____ miles

What is the **minimum** distance possible between City 1 and City 3?

Minimum distance = _____ miles

On the map, draw a picture of all the possible locations of City 3.

City 1   City 2

Scientific Sara!

Sara made a chart of the results of an experiment in her science class. The last entry in the chart got torn off. As she looked at the torn chart, she realized there was a pattern to the results, so she was able to fill in the last two sections.

10	20	40	70	110	160		

What numbers did she write in to complete the chart?

_____

Name _____

Captain Chris is organizing his charts.
Help him complete the charts below.

Complete the following chart:

1 + 2 + 3 + . . .	+ 9 + 10 = 55
1 + 2 + 3 + . . .	+ 99 + 100 = 5,050
1 + 2 + 3 + . . .	+ 999 + 1,000 = 500,500
1 + 2 + 3 + . . .	+ 9,999 + 10,000 = _____
1 + 2 + 3 + . . .	+ 1,000,000 = _____
1 + 2 + 3 + . . .	+ 1_____ = 5,000,050,000

Complete the following chart:

11 x 11 =	121
111 x 111 =	12,321
1,111 x 1,111 =	1,234,321
11,111 x 11,111 =	_____
1,111,111 x 1,111,111 =	_____
_____ x _____	= 12,345,654,321

Explain Yourself!

Name _____

How much is 99 + 99 + 99 + 99?

_____

Explain your answer. _____

_____

_____

How much is 100 + 102 + 104 + 106? _____

Explain your answer. _____

_____

How much is 99 + 120 + 80 + 101? _____

Explain your answer. _____

_____

How much is 300 take away 101? _____

Explain your answer. _____

_____

How much is 100 take away 105? _____

Explain your answer. _____

_____

Wacky Widgets!

Ten widgets cost $2.50. (One widget costs a quarter.)

How much do nine widgets cost? _____

Explain your answer. _____

_____

How much do 12 widgets cost? _____

Explain your answer. _____

_____

How much do 20 widgets cost? _____

Explain your answer. _____

_____

How much do 5 widgets cost? _____

Explain your answer. _____

_____

How much do 30 widgets cost? _____

Explain your answer. _____

_____

Some Like It Hot!

Water freezes at 32 degrees Fahrenheit and boils at 212 degrees.
Water freezes at 0 degrees Celsius and boils at 100 degrees.

How many degrees is it from
freezing to boiling on the
Fahrenheit scale? _____

How many degrees is it from
freezing to boiling on the
Celsius scale? _____

The water in each pan on the stove is exactly the same temperature.
The heat in the pan on the left went up 1 degree Fahrenheit. The
heat in the pan on the right went up 1 degree Celsius.

Which pan now has the hotter water?

Circle one: left pan   right pan

Explain your answer. _____

_____

_____

Others Like It Cold!

Water freezes at 32 degrees Fahrenheit and boils at 212 degrees. Water freezes at 0 degrees Celsius and boils at 100 degrees. (Celsius is also called "centigrade.")

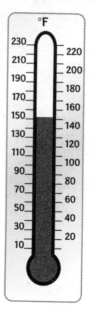

Is 0 degrees Fahrenheit hotter or colder than 0 degrees Celsius?

    Circle one: hotter   colder

Explain your answer. _____

_____

_____

Is "below zero" on the Celsius scale always "below zero" on the Fahrenheit scale? _____

Explain your answer. _____

_____

_____

Halfway between freezing temperature and boiling temperature on the Fahrenheit scale is _____ degrees.

Which Is Heavier?

One kilogram is about 2.2 pounds.

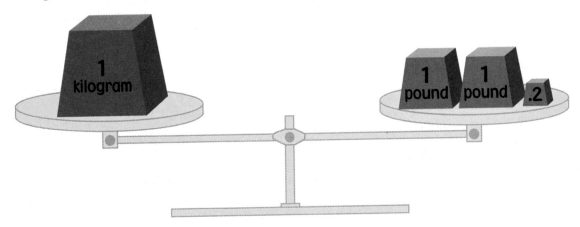

About how many pounds does a 50-kilogram sack of coffee beans weigh? _____

Does a fish that weighs 10 pounds weigh more or less than 5 kilograms?

_____

Is a pound more or less than half of a kilogram?

Circle one: more   less

Explain your answer. _____

_____

_____

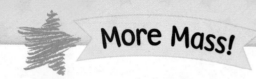

More Mass!

Name _____

Does a 100 kilogram man weigh more or less than 200 pounds? Fill-in the blank with either ">" or "<." Remember, > means "greater than" and < means "less than." _____

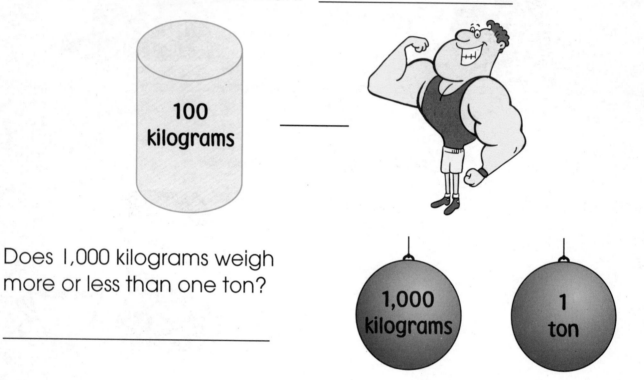

100 kilograms _____

Does 1,000 kilograms weigh more or less than one ton?

_____

1,000 kilograms

1 ton

A penny weighs 2.5 grams. A kilogram is 1,000 grams.

How many pennies must be put on the scale to balance the one kilogram weight? _____

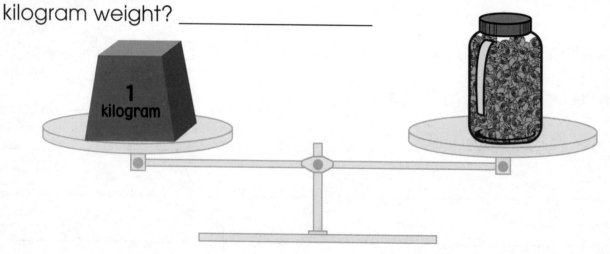

1 kilogram

Rules of the Road

One kilometer is a little more than half of a mile. (1 km = 0.6 miles)

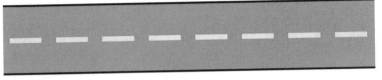

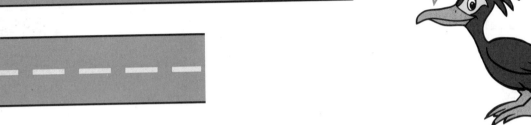

Is 10 kilometers more or less than 5 miles? _____

Two cars start driving from City A to City B. The first car travels at a steady rate of 40 kilometers per hour. The second car travels at a steady rate of 40 miles per hour. Which car gets to City B first?

Circle one: Car 1   Car 2

Is a mile more or less than two kilometers?

Circle one: more   less

Explain your answer. _____

_____

_____

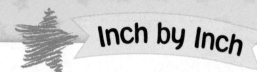
Name _____

One inch is exactly 2.54 centimeters.

One inch is exactly 2.54 centimeters.

1 inch

1 cm.

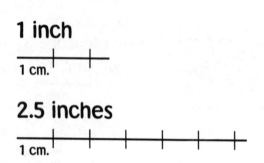

2.5 inches

1 cm.

Is 10 centimeters more or less than five inches? _____

A yard is 36 inches. About how many centimeters is this?

Circle one: 20   40   60   80   100

Is a centimeter more or less than half of an inch?

Circle one: more   less

Explain your answer. _____

_____

_____

Got Milk?

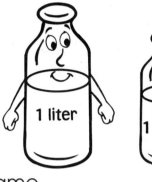

One liter is a little more than one quart.

Four quarts make a gallon.

Which is bigger: two liters or half-a-gallon?

  Circle one: two liters   half-a-gallon   same

Two pints make a cup.

Two cups make a quart.

About how many pints are there in a liter? Remember, a liter is a little more than a quart.

  Circle one: 1 to 2   2 to 3   3 to 4   4 to 5

Explain your answer. _____

_____

_____

Ranch Hands!

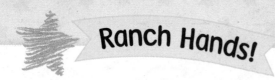

A rancher has 60 yards of fencing to make a corral for some of his horses.

If he makes the corral in a square, how long will each side be? _____

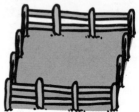

If the corral is in the shape of a rectangle, and the length is 20 yards, how long is the width? _____

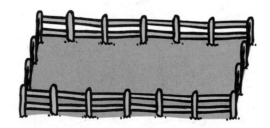

The rancher finally decides to put the corral next to his barn. That way he has to fence in only three sides of it. The long side, which is parallel to the barn, will be 40 yards. How long will each of the other sides be? _____

Name _____

Find the perimeter of a triangle whose sides are 2 inches, $3\frac{1}{2}$ inches, and $4\frac{3}{4}$ inches.

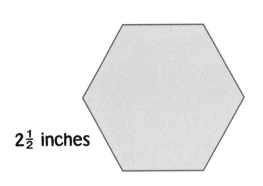

2 inches

$3\frac{1}{2}$ inches

$4\frac{3}{4}$ inches

_____

Find the perimeter of a hexagon whose sides are all $2\frac{1}{2}$ inches.

$2\frac{1}{2}$ inches

_____

Find the length of the side of a square whose perimeter is 30 meters.

perimeter = 30 meters

_____

Find the length of the side of an octagon whose perimeter is 26 feet.

perimeter = 26 feet

_____

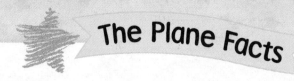

The Plane Facts

Find the area of a square whose sides are each 5 feet.

5 feet

The area of a square is 36 square inches.
Find the perimeter of the square.

area = 36 sq. in.

Which has the greater area: a square
whose sides are each 10 inches or a
circle whose diameter is 10 inches?

Circle one: the square   the circle

10 inches

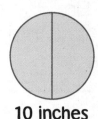

10 inches

The length of the side of a square is doubled.

What is the relationship between the perimeters of the two squares?

Circle one: the perimeters are the same
the new perimeter is twice of the old
the new perimeter is half of the old
the new perimeter is four times the old

What is the relationship between the areas of the two squares?

Circle one: the areas are the same
the new square is twice as big
the new square is half as a big
the new square is four times as big

More Plane Facts

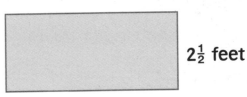

Find the area of a rectangle whose length is 6 feet and whose width is $2\frac{1}{2}$ feet. _____

6 feet

$2\frac{1}{2}$ feet

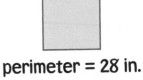

The perimeter of a square is 28 inches. Find the area of the square. _____

perimeter = 28 in.

Which has the greater area: a square whose side is 5 inches or a circle whose diameter is 5 inches?

Circle one: the square   the circle

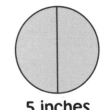

5 inches

5 inches

The three angles of a triangle always add up to 180 degrees.

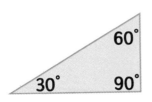

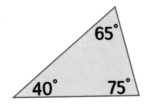

Find the size of each angle if each angle is equal. _____

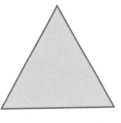

A hexagon can be broken down into four triangles. How many degrees are there in each angle of a hexagon? _____

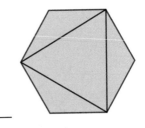

Find the size of each angle if the second is twice the first and the third angle is three times the first.

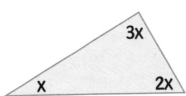

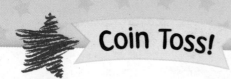

Name _____

Three coins are tossed. Make a list of all the possible combinations of heads and tails that can occur. (Hint: There are **8 ways** that 3 coins can come up.)

_____   _____

_____   _____

_____   _____

_____   _____

This time, 4 coins are tossed. Make a list of all the possible combinations of heads and tails that can occur. (Hint: There are **16 ways** that 3 coins can come up.)

_____   _____

_____   _____

_____   _____

_____   _____

_____   _____

_____   _____

_____   _____

_____   _____

52 Cards

Nick has a regular deck of 52 playing cards.

He picks one card from the deck. How many of the cards are "winners" if he wants the card to be a red card?

_____

  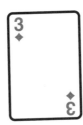   

Nick puts the card he picked back in the deck and picks another card. How many of the cards are "winners" if he wants the card to be a face card (a jack, queen, or king)?

_____

Again he puts the card he picked back in the deck and picks another card. How many of the cards are "winners" if he wants the card to be a prime number (a 2, 3, 5, or 7)?

_____

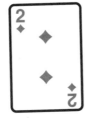 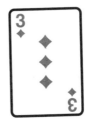 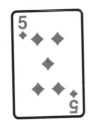 

Fair Share!

Name _____

Martha and George take turns baby-sitting. Martha works for 4 hours and George works for 2 hours. They are paid $24.00. How should they share the money? _____

One ton of sand is to be put into 50-pound bags. Each bag will sell for $5.00. How much is the sand worth? _____

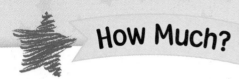
How Much?

A family wants to travel 1,000 miles in four days by car. On the first day, they traveled 275 miles. On the second day, they covered 245 miles. How many miles must they average on **each** of the next two days?

day 1—275 miles
day 2—245 miles
day 3—
day 4—

_____

A girl put $25.00 in the bank. Each week for 12 weeks she deposited $5.50 more. Then she took out $12.75. How much was left in the account? _____

An aquarium is three-fourths full of water. Half of the water leaks out. How full is the aquarium now? _____

Name _____

7 is soooo average!

Find the average of 4, 5, 7, and 12.

_____

Find the average of 10, 15, and 65. _____

The average of three numbers is 15. Two of the numbers are 15 and 10. Find the third number.

15   (15 + 10 + ?) ÷ 3

_____

Michael had an average of 30 points per game for four games. How many total points did he score?

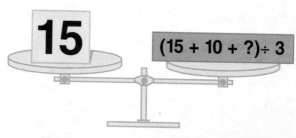

30   (game 1 + game 2 + game 3 + game 4) ÷ 4

_____

Easy as Pie!

Name _____

Shade-in $\frac{1}{2}$ of the first circle.

Shade-in $\frac{2}{4}$ of the first circle.

What is another name for this amount? _____

Shade-in $\frac{3}{4}$ of the first circle.

Shade-in $\frac{4}{4}$ of the first circle.

Shade-in $\frac{7}{4}$.

Shade-in $\frac{5}{4}$.

Shade-in $\frac{8}{4}$.

Shade-in $\frac{6}{4}$.

Shade-in $\frac{11}{4}$.

Easy as Pie—Part II!

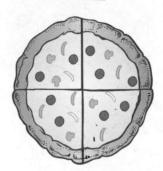

$\frac{3}{4} + \frac{3}{4} =$ _____

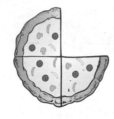
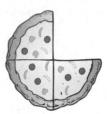

$\frac{3}{4} + \frac{3}{4} + \frac{3}{4} + \frac{3}{4} =$ _____

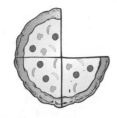
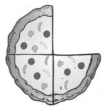
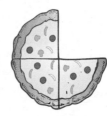
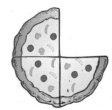

$1\frac{3}{4} + 1\frac{3}{4} =$ _____

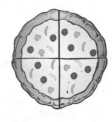
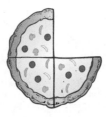
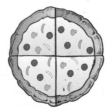
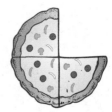

$\frac{1}{4} + \frac{2}{4} + \frac{3}{4} + \frac{4}{4} =$ _____

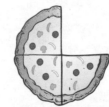
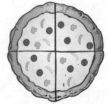

$\frac{1}{4} + \frac{2}{4} + \frac{3}{4} + \frac{4}{4} + \frac{5}{4} =$ _____

Ordering Fractions

Circle all the numbers whose value is **less** than $\frac{1}{2}$:

$0,\quad 1,\quad \frac{1}{2},\quad \frac{3}{8},\quad \frac{5}{7},\quad \frac{1}{10},\quad \frac{7}{8},\quad \frac{5}{7},\quad \frac{2}{9}$

Circle all the numbers whose value is **greater** than $\frac{1}{2}$:

$0,\quad 1,\quad \frac{1}{2},\quad \frac{5}{8},\quad \frac{2}{5},\quad \frac{7}{10},\quad \frac{7}{8},\quad \frac{5}{11},\quad \frac{11}{20}$

Circle all the numbers whose value is **equal to** $\frac{1}{2}$:

$0,\quad 1,\quad \frac{1}{2},\quad \frac{4}{8},\quad \frac{2}{5},\quad \frac{7}{10},\quad \frac{5}{10},\quad \frac{6}{13},\quad \frac{18}{13}$

Arrange in order from **smallest** to **largest**:

$0,\quad 1,\quad \frac{1}{2},\quad \frac{3}{8},\quad \frac{5}{7},\quad \frac{1}{10}$ _____

$0,\quad 1,\quad \frac{1}{2},\quad \frac{3}{5},\quad \frac{4}{9},\quad \frac{9}{10}$ _____

Which is bigger: $\frac{9}{10}$ or $\frac{19}{20}$?

   Circle one: $\frac{9}{10}$ $\frac{19}{20}$

Explain your answer. _____

_____

_____

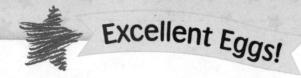

Excellent Eggs!

A dozen eggs cost $1.50.

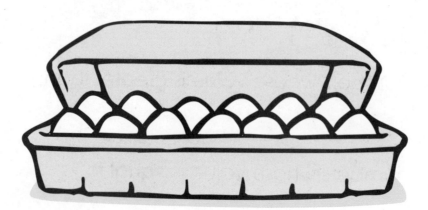

How much do three dozen eggs cost? _____

How much do 60 eggs cost? _____

How much does a half dozen eggs cost? _____

How much does one egg cost? _____

How much does a gross (12 dozen) of eggs cost? _____

How much do 2½ dozen eggs cost? _____

How many eggs can you buy for $6.00? _____

How many eggs can you buy for $9.00? _____

It's Eggy or (Not so Excellent Eggs!)

A dozen eggs cost $1.50.

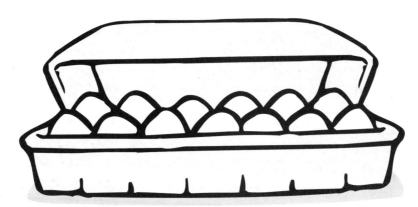

If one-quarter of the eggs are cracked, how many eggs are **not** cracked? _____

If four eggs are cracked, what (fractional) part of the dozen is **not** cracked? _____

A carton of eggs has been dyed. Three eggs are red, four are white, and the rest are blue. If you reach into the carton and take out one egg, what is the probability that it will be blue? _____

What is the probability of pulling out an egg that is **not** red?

_____

The King and the Doctor

One day, a king summoned the royal doctor. The king's son was very sick. "Save my son's life," commanded the king, "and I will give you any amount of money you ask."

After several days, the king's son was restored to health by the doctor. "Thank you, Doctor," said the king. "What do you request as payment?"

"A checkerboard has 8 rows and 8 columns, 64 squares in all. Place I penny on the first square, 2 pennies on the second square, 4 pennies on third square, 8 pennies on the fourth square, and keep doubling, until you reach the 64th square. I will take the amount on the 64th square. This will be payment enough," said the doctor.

The king offered the doctor ten million dollars instead. Should the doctor accept the king's offer? Why or why not?

_____

_____

_____

How much money will be on the 64th square? _____

Star and Stripes Forever!

Each American flag has 50 stars and 13 stripes.

How many **stars** are there in the picture? _____

How many **stripes**? _____

How many **more** flags are needed to have exactly 750 stars?

_____

How many stripes are there on 25 flags? _____

How many flags can be made out of 2,000 stars? _____

Name _____

There is a movie theater with 10 rows of seats. Each row has 15 seats. Tickets to the movie theater cost $6.00 each.

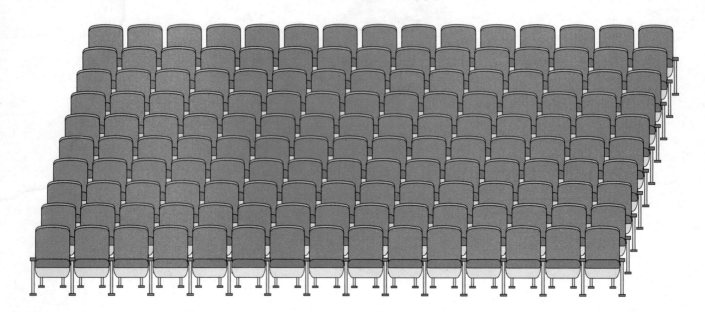

How many total seats are there in the theater? _____

How much money does the theater take in if there is a full house?

_____

How much money does the theater take in if all but the last two rows are filled?

_____

How much money does the theater take in if all but the last $2\frac{1}{3}$ rows are filled?

_____

Answers

Page 5
Answers will vary.

Page 6
Answers will vary.

Page 7
Mercury. Pluto.
240,000; 93,000,000;
483,000,000; 3,700,000,000

Page 8
7; 14; 28; 29; 30; 31; 365;
3,652; 3,653

Page 9
About 70; about 300

Page 10
5,000; 700

Page 11
235, 347, 325, 501; 190, 277,
299, 99; 55, 550, 5, 50

Page 12
8370; 1544; 11,111; 2,765,433;
2344; 726

Page 13
No, he does not have
enough. Estimated $10 +
$20 + $25 = $55
$200 left.

Page 14
390; 290; 800; 540; 1010; 10;
700; 120; 1020; 9020; 1010

Page 15
500; 320; 370; 43,200; 4; 150;
100; 6
98,765,432; 3,210,432

Page 16
1800; 4200; 3000; 36,000
20; 15; 100; 10
333,333,333; 1300

Page 17
5,865,696,000,000
Multiply 60 X 60 X 24 X 365;
drop 3 zeros and multiply it
by 186 (dropped 3 zeros).
When you get the answer,
you add 6 zeros to it.

Page 18
126,720 half-inches
111,111,111; 222,222,222;
333,333,333; 444,444,444;
888,888,888; 45

Page 19
7.56; 9.57; 15.42; 138.67
5.75; 9.55; 2.44; 8.3

Page 20
47.86; 10.94; 3.28; 89.21

Page 21
16, 22, 29; 29, 28, 38; 32, 64,
128; 36, 49, 64; 21, 34, 55; 1;
$\frac{1}{2}$; $\frac{1}{4}$

Page 22
7$\frac{1}{2}$, 9, 10$\frac{1}{2}$; 63, 127, 255; 29,
28, 38; 160, 320, 640; 5, 0, -5;
315, 635, 1275

Page 23
They are all flat figures with
straight lines.
They are all circular
3-dimensional figures.
They are all 3-dimensional
figures.

Page 24
The circle does not belong.
The others are flat figures
with straight lines.
The triangle does not
belong. The others are
three-dimensional.
The circle does not belong.
The others are flat figures
with straight lines.

Page 25
$3.19; $7.78; $18.63

Page 26
$96.70; 20 dimes. Hannah
knows that there are 10
quarters, which equals $2.50
of the total amount. That
leaves $2.00 worth of dimes,
which equals 20 dimes.

Page 27
$62.50; $100.00; $125.00

Page 28
$2.50; $80.00

Page 29
$\frac{1}{4}$; 6; 24 marbles; $\frac{1}{2}$ are now
blue; $\frac{1}{6}$ are now white.

Page 30
$\frac{1}{2}$ mile; $\frac{3}{4}$ mile; $\frac{15}{16}$ mile; 2
furlongs; 9$\frac{1}{2}$ furlongs

Page 31
48 oz. = 3 lbs.; 1100 lbs. of
sand; $\frac{5}{8}$ is left.

Page 32
Papa Bear ate one quarter
of the pie.
Mama Bear ate one quarter
of the pie.
Baby Bear ate one quarter
of the pie.
One quarter of the pie was
left for Goldilocks.

Page 33
The missing number is 11.
The jar was half full on the
19th day.
Freddie is the better shooter.
$\frac{17}{24}$ is better than $\frac{16}{24}$.

Page 34
Maximum distance=125 miles
Minimum distance=75 miles

Page 35
220, 290, 370, 460, and 560

Page 36
50,005,000; 500,000,500,000;
100,000
123,454,321;
1,234,567,654,321; 111,111 X
111,111

Page 37
396. 99 is almost 100, so add
each number to get 400,
then subtract 4.
412. Add the hundreds
place to get 400, then add
ones to get 12.
400. Add 99 and 101 to get
200; then add 120 and 80 to
get 200. Add together to
get 400.
299. 300 minus 100 is 200.
Then subtract one more to
get 199.
-5. 100 minus 100 is 0.
Subtract five more to get –5.

Page 38
Nine widgets cost $2.25.
Multiply $0.25 times 9 to get
your answer.
Twelve widgets cost $3.
Multiply $0.25 times 12 to get
your answer.
Twenty widgets cost $5.
Multiply $0.25 times 20 to get
your answer.
Five widgets cost $1.25.
Multiply $0.25 times 5 to get
your answer.
Thirty widgets cost $7.50.
Multiply $0.25 times 30 to get
your answer.

Page 39
180 degrees Fahrenheit
100 degrees Celsius
Children should circle the
right pan.
The right pan is hotter
because 1 degree Celsius
equals 2.12 degrees
Fahrenheit. Therefore, one
degree Celsius is greater
than one degree Fahrenheit.

Page 40
Children should circle colder.
32 degrees is freezing on the
Fahrenheit scale.
No.
Negative one degree Celsius
is equal to 30.2 degrees
Fahrenheit.
90 degrees is halfway
between freezing and
boiling on the Fahrenheit
scale.

Page 41
110 pounds
Less than 5 kilograms
Children should circle less.
1 kilogram is equal to 2.2
pounds. Half of a kilogram is
equal to 1.1 pounds.
Therefore, one pound is less
than half a kilogram.

Page 42
>
1,000 kilograms equals 2,200
pounds. It weighs more than
one ton.
400 pennies must be put on
the scale to balance the
one kilogram weight.

Page 43
More than 5 miles
Children should circle Car 2, traveling 40 miles per hour.
Children should circle more. One kilometer is equal to .6 miles. Therefore, two kilometers is equal to 1.2 miles. So, I mile is more than two kilometers.

Page 44
Less than
Children should circle 100.
Children should circle less.
Half of an inch is equal to 1.27 centimeters. Therefore, one centimeter is less than half an inch.

Page 45
Children should circle two liters.
Children should circle 4 to 5. There are four pints in a quart. A liter is a little more than a quart. So, 4 to 5 pints are in one liter.

Page 46
15 yards
10 yards
10 yards each

Page 47
10 $\frac{1}{4}$ inches
15 inches
7 $\frac{1}{2}$ meters
3 $\frac{1}{4}$ feet

Page 48
25 feet
24 inches
Children should circle the square.
Children should circle the new perimeter is twice of the old.
Children should circle the new square is four times as big.

Page 49
15 feet
49 inches
Children should circle the square.
60 degrees
120 degrees
30 degrees, 60 degrees, 90 degrees

Page 50
Penny	Nickel	Quarter
heads	heads	heads
heads	heads	tails
heads	tails	heads
tails	heads	heads
heads	tails	tails
tails	heads	tails
tails	tails	heads
tails	tails	tails

Penny	Nickel	Dime	Quarter
heads	heads	heads	heads
heads	heads	heads	tails
heads	tails	heads	heads
heads	heads	tails	heads
tails	heads	heads	heads
tails	tails	tails	tails
heads	tails	tails	tails
tails	heads	tails	tails
tails	tails	heads	tails
tails	tails	tails	heads
tails	tails	heads	heads
tails	tails	heads	heads
heads	heads	tails	tails
tails	heads	heads	tails
heads	tails	tails	heads
heads	tails	heads	tails
tails	heads	tails	heads

Page 51
26 cards
12 cards
16 cards

Page 52
Martha should get 16 dollars, and George should get 8 dollars.
The sand is worth $200.

Page 53
They must cover 240 miles on each day.
$78.25 was left in the account.
It is $\frac{1}{4}$ full.

Page 54
The average is 7.
The average is 30.
The third number is 20.
He scored a total of 120 points.

Page 55
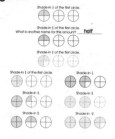
Shade-in $\frac{1}{2}$ of the first circle.
What is another name for this amount? **half**

Page 56
$\frac{6}{4}$ or 1$\frac{1}{2}$
$\frac{12}{4}$ or 3
2$\frac{6}{4}$ or 3$\frac{1}{2}$
2$\frac{1}{2}$
$\frac{15}{4}$ or 3$\frac{3}{4}$

Page 57
$\frac{3}{8}$, $\frac{1}{10}$, $\frac{2}{9}$
0, 1, $\frac{5}{8}$, $\frac{7}{10}$, $\frac{7}{8}$, $\frac{11}{20}$
$\frac{1}{2}$, $\frac{4}{8}$, $\frac{5}{10}$
0, $\frac{4}{9}$, $\frac{1}{2}$, $\frac{3}{5}$, $\frac{9}{10}$, 1
0, $\frac{1}{10}$, $\frac{3}{8}$, $\frac{1}{2}$, $\frac{5}{7}$, 1
Children should circle $\frac{19}{20}$.
To compare the fractions, give each fraction a common denominator of 20. $\frac{9}{10}$ becomes $\frac{18}{20}$, which is less than $\frac{19}{20}$.

Page 58
$4.50
$7.50
$0.75
About $0.13
$18
$3.75
48 eggs
72 eggs

Page 59
9 eggs aren't cracked.
$\frac{2}{3}$ aren't cracked.
There is a $\frac{5}{12}$ of a probability the egg will be blue.
There is a $\frac{9}{12}$ or $\frac{3}{4}$ probability the egg will not be red.

Page 60
The doctor should not accept the king's offer. After square 23, you're already over the $10 million.
Extra credit:
The amount on the 64th square is 9,223,372,036,854,775,808 cents (9 quintillion cents) or $92,233,720,368,547,758.08 (92 quadrillion dollars).

Page 61
There are 500 stars in the picture.
There are 130 stripes in the picture.
5 more flags are needed for 750 stars.
There would be 325 stripes on 25 flags.
40 flags can be made out of 2,000 stars.

Page 62
150 seats total
$900
$720
$690